River Bed

Poems and Prose

Andrea L. Weiser

Manufactured in the United States of America through Lulu.com.

Cover art: Watercolor, "Jordan Creek," by Don Smith. Handmade felt by Cherie Donovan-Smith

Cover photo (back) by Rachel R. W. Robertson

Prior publication: First North American print rights for the following works contained in this book were sold or given to other publishers:

"Wet Behind the Ears," to *American Whitewater* (1996)
"Highway Roses," to *Images Magazine* (1991)
"After Love Soup — the Never Again," and "Memory Cup," and "The Cold Hardiness of Vegetables," to *Kinesis* (1993)
"Filament" to *Prism* (1991)
"Forty-seven Miles," to *Roofbeam* (1998)
"Bedding Down" to *Surviving the Western State of Mind: A Montana Writer's Daybook* (1996)
"Dakota Prairie" and "Fighting Fire with a Pulaski and a Smile," to *The Tracker* (1996)

Upon the first printing of these works, all rights reverted back to the author and it is the author's sole right to reprint them.

Dedication

To my grandmother, Ruth Jensine Weiser.

In the dream, my grandmother looked at me in the dim light
and told me with her eyes she would die soon.
"Oh," she said, absently, "did I give you the river?"
I narrowed my eyes, trying to discern what she meant.

In silence she drew me outside and we looked down on the
water — rippling and shimmering in the dark — and we listened
to its gurgle and hiss.

"Did I give you the river?" she whispered. This time her eyes
were insistent, and her words struck a deeper chord in me. A
wise woman was handing me knowledge like a stone — I could
feel the weight of it.

It was spring thaw and the water was high and murky with silt,
crushing its banks with substance and passion. I could smell it
and feel the river pulsing below us like the heartbeat of a wild
animal. I knew this was important, I just didn't know why.

She lived into September.

Grandmother, these words are from my *river bed*.

Contents

Prose

Lessons From Ruth

Don't be afraid when the raven comes to get you,
and you follow to a familiar place you've never been.
Don't be afraid when the reel of your life rolls back
and you only speak Norwegian.

When your hands are young again,
and everyone is calling.
You stack up your accomplishments
by the blood in your children, and feel proud
about the generations to come.

The words leave you completely
because there is a different language now,
but you teach your children
how to speak it with their hands.

That is how you die.

Upriver Spring

The Skagit River breaks her banks,
like a tight whip against the back of a mare.

The canyons yawn and rumble,
electrified with waterfalls.

Narrow creek beds talk across the river
in the old way.

Up in the teeth of the mountains
snow melts between tongues of warmth.
Snow bridges dissolve like sugar candy.
Glaciers sing in whispered voices.
Crevices open, and shadows look like shapes.

Glacier pebbles wash into channels and ride.
They tumble through the roar and the quiet,
drawn to the river, like magnets.

Frothy creeks pulse through slot canyons,
ploughing bedrock in their wake —
hell bent for big water.

The Skagit works her banks,
earth-moving with persistence.
Creeks carve their routes and join her,
murmuring with relief.

The Skagit flows fast and quiet underneath.
On top, the waves roll hushed and easy.
She moves along with a smile.
down river, down valley, she lays on her belly.
She spreads out thin on soft tilled acres.
She pools up in cultivated fields
where tulips quicken.

Glacier Country

Sunrise glows over mountain's back
like a shallow dream.
There is no name for this color.
Not yellow. Not gold.
Awakening. A raw energy pulsing forward
with sleepy feet—
that is daybreak.

Filament

The kiss was more than touching lips,
it was the end of just friends and the beginning of a dream.
No one could say, "I didn't mean that,"
like it is in the movies.
We were stuck in the us we just made.

The web stuck to our skin.
We remembered being sucked up by the spider before.
Don't blame me for the thread.
Your lips moved too.
Spider is not hungry for us.
We are one bundle — love and hate crossing over and back
winding us deeper.

Our lips remember when to kiss and when to speak.
Threads tighten and connect us.
Our hearts know this dream never ends.
The spider just hovers.

Crocus

My heart took a journey through the wilderness.
It has been a long time since I felt my soul travel.
The trees taught me about wind.
The stone whispered, "water."
My mother said, "don't be afraid to try."

Space and time made room for me.
My heart came back.

It is always good to understand
the small moments of the universe.
This day, I saw the center of a crocus blossom
and cried with gratitude.

What the Aspen Said

The aspen leaves rattle
like hard pellets of rain on rock slabs.

Air tastes of snow
that rolls across my tongue like a cool drink.

The tree seduces me to move close.

I hear other-world sounds,
like the rough cough of a truck engine
as it labors to breathe winter air.
My prejudiced ears push these sounds distant
as I listen to a young aspen tree talk excitedly of winter.

The lemon-hued leaves dance on limber red stems —
a staccato motion,
expressing their hearts out until they drop to stillness.
It is not a sad dance, but a celebration.

I glide my hand on the smooth pressed bark.
I can hardly feel the surface with touch.
Instead, I feel the insides.
Like laying a hand on the heart of a friend.

Aspen and wind continue to engage
in conversation about winter.
The world will be simple and defined by cold.
Frost-licked leaves will turn brown as coffee,
and let go.

Black crow gleams as if dipped in magic
and turns a circle, ceremoniously, on chilled air.

Glacier Bed

My fingers long to touch the untouchable—a glacier.
My fascination grows as I feel the slow
and powerful presence—like an elephant, or a tower of stone.
The vibration is quieter than a whisper,
only the ears of my soul can hear.

What would it be like to lay down in its rhythm?
To feel myself ice?
Each crystal shifts and hums at a rate I cannot perceive.
Surface mass balance—a sleepy response to solar coaxing.
a long yawn through winter storms.

One snowflake falls.
One, small, delicate slice of humidity.
One snowflake, then another, and another,
interlocking, laying down a bed of change.
The bed of a glacier, stacks up like a frozen wall
on the back of a continent.

Oscillations from the ocean call to the mountains,
the ice answers.
And what of the moon's call to ice, water, and air?
One snowflake falls, and another, interlocking,
laying down a deep rhythm that quickens now
as summer draws near.

There is a place I know, where the ice calves off the mountain,
shakes the sky, and tips boulders like teacups.
I tremble in that sound that cracks the world.
These stones, so long under ice, roll down the mountain
and find the lick of river.
These stones have slept through our ancestry
and now find their way in our future.

Backs Touching

Between the hours of eleven and midnight,
I lay awake remembering how you never held me in sleep.

You loved me with words but not touch.
You loved me with praise but your acts contradicted.
All that time I could sustain us on memories and beginnings—
the courting dance, the kiss when all our doubts fell away.

Tears dry tight lines on my cheeks
but your presence would give no comfort.
Your stormy breathing and the rising of your back
fed loneliness.
There was so much sheet between us—like an empty plate.

Dawn at Summer Land

Sun rises over Crystal Ridge,
sending a rosy glow across the canyon,
like an echo, to the top of Tahoma.

Glacier-fed streams continue their healthy chatter,
through talus slopes and mountain goat trails,
over boulders and around purple islands of monkey flowers.

The light changes on the mountain.
Rose, to gold, to white.
The crowns of alpine firs are kissed with light.

Subalpine tundra—
gold, green, and salted with white blossoms of yarrow.

The hangnail moon is luminous
against a dim blue September sky.

The haze of smoke beds down in the valleys,
tendrils rising up from the eastern flank of the Cascades.

A lone marmot grazes in the tundra,
belly pressing a trail through mountain asters.

The sun nears the crest of Crystal Ridge
illuminating wisps of cirrus clouds and one glowing contrail
from a jet heading east.

Fish Dance

Jade river —
deliciously silver where riffles break.

Paddle-backed salmon
align themselves in deep water
to rest.

River whispers across cobble bars
and slides along logs
between branches.

Cottonwood leaves rattle together.
Gold ones drop from branch to branch.
Slap, flutter, slap.

The fish dance is a haphazard ballet.
Loosening their eggs with mild desperation.
Slap, flutter-flutter-flutter.
Slap. SLAP!
Lives depend on it.

They breach like dolphins.
Leap like trout.
Flap like broken-winged birds.

Some jump in sets.
Underneath they ease back into position.
They meditate.
They fast.

Focus. Wait.
Re-align. Begin.

After Love Soup — the Never Again

I came out of the deep waters dripping and near-drown.
It was so cold, like ice touching my skin
and breaking every cell before all went numb.
I vowed to never fall into the deep again.
I would only walk the shallows —
Perhaps up to the mid-calf or knee,
but never to the thigh, or hip, or under.
The swimming was too much, the treading,
the going without air or senses.

No. Swimming was out.

No more tangling in the water weeds and being sucked under
in the murk. Certainly, no enduring waves and headwinds.
That was in the past.

Only my feet need touch the curling lip of waves.
Just the toes. The very ends, that's all.

Big Water

One fall day, when I walked the tight rope of a log,
Redoubt Creek gushed and hammered below me
like a freight train to Little Beaver Creek.

I thought of my ancestor, Conrad Weiser,
facing the gush of spring thaw alone
on the Indian trail to the Mohawk village.
What a strange man he must have been
to all who knew him — even his wife.

He was a man of solitude and a man of purpose;
carrying messages of nations in shell wampum belts,
learning his way past the obstacles of language and etiquette,
forging through high water, darkness,
hunger that made him reach for divine guidance.
Fear. Starvation. Delirium. Acceptance.
Some of these I know by heart.

I saw four bears that day. Their noses were deep
in berry bushes, hackles high, as I passed through their kitchen.
The spiders were busy throwing their nets across the gap of
trail.

And what about Peter Weiser, pulling his weight
for Captains Lewis and Clark?
He must have had the skills desired to crack the code
of wilderness. A strong back, an eager temperament.
He was so young at the start and so old at the end.

When I set out on the trail of intentions,
my pack loaded with provisions,
I think of the Weisers before me,
carrying the hope of adventure on their hearts
as they embarked on what was sure to be
their closest brush with death and surest way to be alive.

Bedrock

In the spring,
I find a flat rock with a good disposition.
I speak to it with my fingers.
I lie down on it.

The sun warms my winter skin
and I listen to the river
sing of creation.

After Harvest (the seed tree)

She stood like a dancer—
her toes pointed to the earth,
her limbs elegantly stretching to the sky.

How wonderful to be alive
even in these times.
To be the chosen one
to seed another generation of green beauties.

But who will teach them the lessons of trees?
How will they learn to speak
without coaxing through the roots?

They will reinvent the songs of centuries while she wanes.
They will speak the language underground,
while she diminishes.

April Flowers

Tenuous winds shift winter's sleep,
dormancy nudged free by leaf bud clusters shyly advancing.
Then the buds, the fruits of spring, lean open quietly —
coaxed by wild bird melodies.

Petals of azalea rise to the outer rhythm.
Pressing forth into the air, they suspend
like bright crowns balanced on each branch.

Delicate, robust, and blithe, they animate our vision.
They urge a smile each year.
Perspective is enlightened.
Footsteps lighter.
Spring advances like a promise
that joy is possible.

Floating

Your image visits me,
visits the empty canoe of my heart.

It is not quite broken, but it floats on the river
with nothing to guide it.

My heart will rest a while, without passengers.
Float a while — empty.

Unspoken

The air was storm air—charged, and unpredictable.
I could feel the rise of fine hairs on my neck
and my ears grew hot from apprehension.

Your words passed through me like lead,
then reverberated back
like a brass church bell in the lonesome distance.

We are over, you said. This is it.
I noticed the rhythm your lips made, but not your talk.
Your lips were tight against your teeth.
No need to consult your eyes for referral.
The bell had sounded.

Hollowly, I voiced my agreement.
Quietly, you walked away,
as if nothing had passed between us—
as if we weren't there at all
in the same space.

Highway Roses

Roses faded from her cheeks.
The blood drew back like tide,
with currents of the spirit.

His drinks decided her death.
The fate of her children.
he was young.

The man who held her had to let her go.
He gave the boy a chance at life
as his daughter faded too.

He could be so strong
because laughter wasn't in him.
It had gone with the roses
on that dark highway near St. Cloud.

(Anger)

A lump of argument lies in my throat.
I cast down my eyes so as not to burn lasers
across your face.

Your words dare me, but I wait
for the heat on the ends of my ears to draw back
to center.

Forgiveness. Love. Forgiveness.

Autumn Moon

Prime fruit has overstepped time.
Darkness falls and wine is in the leaves.
Children sleep as the chill thickens with October's breath.

Breathe, the oak-apple must.
Say goodbye and let death turn under
to cleanse your path.

Bedding Down

The moon casts her milk shadow
while I listened to an opera of crickets singing
in tongues of love, love lost, tragedy, and deception.
Such is life in these birch woods.
there is nothing simpler or more deft.

There is nothing quieter than grass lying on itself —
a tight matrix our bodies crush down
as we press into each other and turn
to look at the sky.

Forty-seven Miles

Snow fell like teacups on Lizardhead Pass.
The space was cold between us, but we tried.
The cavern opened up, to our relief.
I could see us getting buried by snow, and lost.

No one passed our tracks that night.
In the five times I came close to dying,
This was the most sublime — the lullaby of snow,
tension firm as violin strings,
and the music of Winston carving out a piece of our hearts.

When the sky opened up we knew we had lived,
and lost. We had to admit an end.
Pretending never works in love.
We could agree on that.

Music and Tears

Winthrop; a place that smells like black leather, exhaust,
and spilled stout at the Little Red Pub.
People sleepy from last night's dancing —
the beat still murmuring inside them like reverberations
of Liberty Bell.
Gateway to the North Cascades; waters shimmering and slick,
raging with anger and passion,
pumping like pistons of music
under the cool, open, diamond sky.

Winthrop;
A sound like two words not quite said,
But joined to make one word not quite whole.
Suspended.
Freefalling.

Between the Rivers

The traveler came to this place to rest.
This place between the waters.
This place on Mother's back.

The traveler touched this rock
with soft hands and tender feet,
and hunger made awareness reach the sky.

The traveler sat for days, and listened.

Blues Gone West

In the red dawn of blurred spotlights, the slide guitar wails
to sympathetic brush strokes under Marlboro fog.
Bar-room etiquette prevails above the pic and jab
of western blues,
"Just give me a chance, baby. I'll be anyone you need."
Red lipstick lips and wig hair turns heads of men
who practice lines but never speak—
pull on dancing shoes that never touch the floor.
That's why they are alone.

Longhair swallows lager foam and says to his woman with no
sleeves, "deep."
She turns to him and smiles.
It's really just a man making noise for a buck
but she closes her eyes anyway and tries to ignore that part.

When she was young, the blues were real;
Big Tate would wail on the harp so hard
that tears would sear her eyes just listening.
His face was agony, his song was gruff and poor,
Defiant and beat.
She imagined it was still like that
somewhere east—if anyone cared.

Books

Rough-cut pages bend between finger and thumb.
In this age of screen savers my fingers want to touch trees
flattened out and stacked in bindings.

I can't see the life of a poem
when the cursor pulses at the edge of a line.
Hurry up, it beckons. Over and over.

I can only see stanzas as animals
when they're lined up on parchment
Like starlings scattered over white sky.
Words hang like gliding birds
in shapes that make the poem more than sound and insight.

I can drift somewhere else,
as the book closes on my hand.
I can feel the heaviness of it—the slight grit of paper.
Words spin out from the page,
tangible blocks of ink.

What did the scribe feel when he put down his tools?
Did he keep practicing curves in the dark?
Did he miss the smell of papyrus
when he hung the pages up to dry?

Memory Cup

Storm washes like a whisper over fragile hills.
Grey velvet sky draped in night.
The cricket's chirp and song, a serenade
for garden herbs, and my ears, as I wait.
Flashes burst and melt into velvet
as the secret brews.

Storm caresses the mountain
where we once slept in June.
The old stove we stoked with lodgepole
surely shivers now.
Our miles in candlelight and musk
have stretched distant.
The memory cup is full.

July was born and passed away,
as I waited for your touch.
August now begins and passes by.
I listen to the storm speak of secrets.
If only I could drink memories from your lips.

From the Road

As morning stirs and mist lifts its gloves,
junipers sting the air with intensity,
as wet and green as your eyes, as fresh as your touch.

Think of me as you brush my clothes aside to iron your shirts;
as you smell my spice in the closets and cupboards.
Think of me as you look through lace curtains toward the pines.

I think of you in that moment between sleeping and waking
when everything is still, and junipers whisper
secrets of your eyes.
I think of you as red-tails dance in spirals,
flirting ever deeper as we once did in June.

River Talk

I went down to the river to hear what she had to say.
There was talk of clarity, change, and the persistence of time.

Salmon are ending their life cycle.
The decay is faint in the air, and curiously fresh in its way.

Salmon have taught us lessons for centuries,
about coming home, focus, persistence.
They meditate in the delirium of water
that pushes against them.
Their bodies scrape against the beds of rivers and creeks.
They move as one, yet each journey is solo.

How can we not learn from this greatness?
How can we not see the wisdom of simplicity?
The river speaks it to my eyes and my heart.

Crystal Limericks

In the pale wash of December light
I read poetry on the trees.

Crystals formed by the breath of frost stood still
and brittle. The poem is shrill.
ice tendrils screech for release
from winter's frigid touch.

Over hill, the white snow dollops roll thick as cream.
Serene, innocent white that quiets all sounds.
It comforts my eyes,
and my ears hear the trees no more.

Goose Rock at Deception Pass

A rock staircase for giants leads up
to the top of this damp castle.
Plush runners of moss adorn the landings
in pea-green shag.

Fern plumes and ghostly baby's breath lichens
perch on the furniture in surprising bouquets.

Tapestries in steel grey, dusk, silver frost and cherry
hang askew in open halls of andesite.

Madrona chandeliers are dimly lit with red berries.
Their slick jungle-green leaves are jeweled with water crystals.

Musicians tune their instruments —
a trill, a squeak, a thump, a throaty rasp.
I wait in hushed awe.

From the turret, a kingdom lies open and wet.
A world of ships and sea dragons.
A great lens of water bows the horizon.

Below me, the land is mounded
like a rumpled pile of rugs.

Conversation

"Light beams," he said, with a smile,
eyeing my spun hair.

I can only trust a man as far as I can throw him,
so I'm working on my muscles.

"Freckles like constellations…"

Some say that men and women can't be friends,
but I say they can—until someone mentions she's celibate.

"Elegant hands."

If there was ever a time I needed somebody,
It was that night, and of course nobody was available—
Not for me.

"Skin softer than I've ever touched."

I spent some time trying to find myself,
then suddenly it hit me—
I was underneath him all the while.

"Eyes the color of ocean."

I should have cheated on him first, I suppose,
but it wouldn't have gained me anything.

"Did I tell you, I love you?"

Hey, can we watch the war movie?
Wait, this channel is better.
I like to learn how animals think
so I can understand men better.

Laying Eggs

It is early September.
The Chinook are running.
I go to the river.

It is my woman-time so I put my magic in the water.
I say my prayers as it rolls off my back.

The women come here to lay our eggs in the sand.
Grandmother, help me to believe in it.

A Chinook's belly slaps the water each time I doubt.

I remember being under there,
by the rocks, looking for a place.

Chinook slaps the river.
Merganser stretches her neck out, making soft sounds.
Her wingtips lap the water,
her white bars flash signals.

They are under there
finding a place to make everything begin.

I sit on the dry sand —
sun so kind, breeze light as feathers.
I wish I could breathe underwater once more.

But, here I sit. The water talks in a different way,
The wind walks around my back,
and I am hungry instead of full.

I am hopeful I will find the place.
The right place.
I will lay it down when the time comes.

Inseparable Silence

I still live in the box you left empty
after all our moves.
Accidental snowflakes drifted, effortlessly
into our cold war—
Our locked space,
where no one listens
and no one replies.

Deep Thunder

Thunder rumbles distant.
Branches of lightening illuminate the sky through paned glass.
Rain pelts tin with an uncanny rhythm
deep in the heart.

The sky is a dark veil stretched. Shattered
by fragments of light—the rumble follows in four beats.
The horizon roars.

My heart rests. My breath takes in storm air;
sweet wet grass and tangy earth,
the freshness of maple leaves.
It is all fresh—a taste in the mouth.
My tongue yearns for the taste of storm.
Thirst in my throat.

Let the storm wash away
what was cracked and stubborn.
like dry earth on worn leather, go with the rain.
Dissolve.

It's all part of a dream I never remember upon waking.
In consciousness, dreams are gone
until they happen, and memory connects back
to hazy sleep.

The dream is there in the storm.
In the heart.
Deep like a rhythm of water on tin.
Water music pulls something out,
like lightening pulling out of the veil—
making room for light and energy
that hovered beneath.

Fair Land

The smell of her made him dream
about meadows every night.
He could never quite remember
what he had figured out in sleep.
He only knew she smelled like grass,
and he wanted to wake up next to her skin.

Four Poems

Cat

She crawled on her belly
to go dying among the leaves,
only to find, after much suffering,
four kittens nuzzling her cheeks.

Winter

The windmill stopped
when I thought of you.
No wind, and the doors were open,
revealing a quiet hollow yard
that was always locked before.

Sky Song

In every cathedral of trees,
the wild songs of birds remind us how to live;
simply, and with grace.

You?

One day I looked up and there you were—
greeting me with your eyes,
daring me.

Last Word

Insistent river,
always pushing down the throat
of the valley.

Talking hard on stones
then whispering, silky.

All night,
and day,
and in between the two.

Big talk,
that should stop us all in our tracks.

Harbor Angels

I dreamt of angels above the harbor
where oysters bay.

I dreamt of the sea and evergreens
and the smell of things.

The rain pattered like little feet,
wooing my sleep.

If I could believe in anything,
angels would be good.

They floated with beams of light through sea fog
proving they could find my way,
even if I couldn't.

Little Soda Canyon

Little canyon
touches me deeply

Whispers shush, shush
on the wings of a canyon wren.

The green of spring at the center
wakes thirst in my throat
and aches my heart with thankfulness.

Love Like a Mountain

She walked out and he was left alone with the room talking to him. She had pictures of her loved ones on the walls—the ocean at Yaquina Head lighthouse, Oregon; the rolling drumlins of the Tobacco Plains, Montana; Washington Pass in spring and summer; Pleasant Lake, Minnesota; Little Soda Canyon and Battleship Rock, in the Mesa Verde backcountry. There were no framed faces, just the backbones of ridges, the bellies of hills, canyons that looked like heartwood.

After studying these several times over he realized what it all meant. She could never love him as much as a landscape. No mortal could be what she wanted—as powerful as ocean, as passionate as storm, as loving as desert, as replenishing as river. These were her loves. He knew this. Actually he had known all along in the back of his mind, but he always thought if she would accept him a little at a time he might get under her skin.

Maybe she couldn't love him like a mountain,but maybe like high plains desert, or an unnamed lake. Maybe he could be a favorite stream to her. In return he didn't even know what he wanted or what he might get. With her, there was always a certain way of doing things he was never quite sure of. No pushing. No pulling. No expectations or demands. Sometimes he couldn't even express because he feared she would shut him out. Yet, he loved her.

There was no reasonable explanation and there didn't have to be. She gave him cause to live, to fight, to play. And she listened to him in a tender, undistracted way like no one else. He had never been listened to his whole life, until her.

Lovers

At night,
the river is a woman in a gossamer gown.

The wind pulls her hips into waves
with cool fingertips.

The moon glows over her tight body
like flames.

She slips through the rocks to the sea —
past the river banks that kiss her sides.

She swims on
to her lover at the delta.
She craves his salt touch,
his curling lips bending back to meet her rivulets.
His coveting that rips her waves to silence.

She drags the earth along
so he will see her coming.
She feels his breath swirling,
pushing up her body like mist.

Marriage (for breakfast)

My heart has soured
from so many times warmed up, gone cold,
and warmed up again.

What sustenance I want most
I cannot have—
one man, one love,
like porridge and cream I could breakfast on
and never go hungry.

Passion could go dim without remark
if only I had a bowl that never felt empty,
and a love that would stick to the ribs.

Monarch

Fall butterfly shakes off the chill.
Frayed wings,
still bright with summer's glory.

Nectar scarce,
like a few drops of water
in the bottom of a glass.

Moore Point Orchard

I stood in an orchard of scorched apple trees,
pears, walnuts.
The smell of char stung the back of my throat.

Fruit hung in shriveled clusters.

Parchment paper leaves dangled like fragile mobiles.

There wasn't much time for my task—
mapping the damage of wildfire on a cultural landscape—
but I stood, transfixed, on moon dust.

My Sweet Myalgia Lily

Spider fingers poised on petal's flesh.
The pale, pale skin and vibrant red silk contrast.
A lovely lithe body under silk withers,
yet the heart is lily-strong, fresh, young.

Eyes downcast cloak fear.
The next neck-twisting pain and blur are sure to come,
but the lily-heart wishes it away for seconds more.

She is strength in a fragile shell.
Spider fingers starve for warmth and touch,
but trust died with the last bygone affair.

Now the lily curls to her stem in pale delicacy,
exposing her center, never touched.

Poetic Compromise

The words you spoke into my skin
indelibly rest
like two outstretched cats
who agree to share the same space of sunlight
for the sake of fulfillment.

Olympic Cove

Ocean insists upon sand,
pebbles laughing to the bottom.

Peach-stained sky over glass.
Clouds rise
like dolphins' backs.

Harbor seals
slide off of Cake Rock
and blink inquisitive eyes
in the salty murk.

A sea otter rolls on her back
tapping an oval stone on shell
against her belly.

Foam tickles between stones.
The tide quickens,
the glow dims in the fire.

Gray persists.

Parking-lot Pompadours

Quail scuttle like leaves in the filtered autumn light,
dropping gravel in their gullets and scurrying in
figure eights like ants.

Instinct keeps them scrambling in their covey,
tiptoeing in the open.

They cock their feathered heads to an odd sound, a movement
that isn't wind. A feline tail flutters rapidly, orange and striped.
Tom-cat gathers up his body like a spring.

The covey parts and scatters like prairie fire
across the graveled lot.

A flame of orange fur lopes behind them — duped.
He drops to the ground, watching them
flutter beyond his grasp.
He lowers his head to sniff their trail.

Preparation for Knowing

Building a sweat lodge.
Building a drum.
Building a future.
Building a past.
Tugging against the center.

The poles go deep down
and connect every thing.

The dirt gets packed down and solid
from dancers' feet.

Does everything have more meaning?

Do the songs say something backwards
we can only hear from the inside out?

The marks on our skin keep talking, don't they, uncle?
Brush, brush the fear away.

Brush, brush.
Get the sweat lodge ready.
Our scars are still talking to the tree.

Receiving Wisdom

Water ouzel,
darting through water I cherish.
Cold envelope of familiarity.
Liquid world.
The ballet of sustenance is your hourly dance.

Dull waxy plumage could not be more perfected.
The roar of water your audience, in wild appreciation.

I pull my coat snug across my back. I watch.
I put my mind in your delicate bones.
Every precious millimeter of feather, flesh, and bone,
every sensation of living in both worlds.

I can feel right down to the scales of my feet
that you are my teacher.
My spirit guide
through the fluidity of living.

River Orphans

The aspens wave their naked arms.
The mountains are thirsty for snow.

The sky is no longer a window, it is a sheet;
a gray sheet they are all familiar with —
even the mountain crests that sharpen their teeth for winter.

The autumn smell is the same too —
everything radiates it.
The wind shakes it loose
and pushes down the valleys with it.

The creeks make a racket now that the sky is dim,
and the fire of aspen leaves has snuffed out.

The creeks talk, talk, talk,
like orphans wishing for mothers.

There is a highway up there.
It snakes through the mountains,
fat in the summer and skin and bones in winter —
fragile — like a silver moon.

The road can hear the gossip in Telluride,
and the tic, tic, tic, of a lone aspen leaf
all at the same time.

That one leaf has freckles on it.
Sort of an ugly leaf that hangs on.
All the pretty ones are down below, and still yellow
like banana skins.

The ugly one hangs on by a stem
And goes brown, like a stiff cup of coffee.

Ridgeback

On a wind-licked landscape,
when the wind stops,
all hold their breath.

Lupines loose their pods and turn pale—
watercolor.

Blinding buckskin hills rasped round.
Wind dances across them on tip toes.

Silver beads rest
on the pale back of a birch leaf.

Clouds like flat grey silk
with clean, gilded edges.

Aspen greets loam
with a bouquet of blackened bronze petals—
wet, slick, shaped like hearts.

Jagged cracked pebbles, slate scattered
across slopes like bread crumbs.

Tall pine—
four times my height—
knife crack through your middle.
Branches without fingertips.
Iridescent lichen, like sea urchins,
cling to your wrists.

Sound twitches.

Science and Poetry

Volumes stare down their opposition across the aisle,
bindings wrapped in canvas; brown and blue and green.
Like soldiers, tight in their ranks, firm in stance
against cold white metal shelves.
Call numbers label them like dog tags.
They stand erect, vying for attention of readers who walk the
narrow, green-carpeted line between armies.

The energy crept under my collar from behind
as I browsed the *Iowa Review*. I turned
to see the impending blood-red volumes:
SCIENCE, a series throbbing with history,
bindings cracked and torn,
the oldest beckoned with strength,
seducing my eyes to read the date, 1904.
I touch the grand binding with moist hot fingers.
I even opened it.

But the science I want is enchanted.
The evolution of human thought—
creamy with vague uncharted significance.
Expression that stimulates grey-matter
through rich adaptations of metaphor.
Poetry is victorious.

September 19th

Wind kicks up memories—
the air is stiff and smells like pumpkins.
Winter lays her skirts across the peaks and waits.

I remember turning, spinning as a little girl
crossing autumn streets with a large ladybug
under one arm. Oak leaves quivered like fingers,
ready to drop.

What was her name, the woman who held my hand?
Crossing campus streets, she sent quietness through my fingers.
She watched me stare at things she couldn't see.
We were dwarfed among bricks, steel and concrete.
The giants of St. Paul, trapped in a grid, towered.

We wandered at my pace, her gait slightly crouched
to meet my smallness.
She felt bad, I knew, about my mother.
She hoped to buffer the pain.

She didn't see me walk with ghost feet,
half in her world, half in the other.
She didn't see my mother either,
lilting above us like airborne feathers.

Simple Things

Little old woman bending her spirit back to pick cherries,
groping with juice-stained fingers for the soft ones.

Little woman scrawling, in shaky hand, the names of birds
in the willow branch that drapes across the pond.

Woman in the night, looking up, counting stars,
thinking in ovoid forms.

Dreaming last night's left-over dreams.
Traveling in space. Flying without her body.
Talking in shapes.

Skies

Even where the Colorado carved her routes—
before earth sucked her up and left white powder.
Even there, where our feet leave tracks on soil castles
and the grasses crunch to dust,
where the slick rock molds to our traverses
and ancient culture spreads thin with every wash of rain.
There, the sky is still the same
as nothing else is under foot.

Sky Tears and Ragweed

One hundred dollars for a name.

Grey threads of rain streak to the horizon.
South Dakota stretches flat and colorful like a rag rug—
thin and fresh like pine needles.
Hay stacked like bread loaves turns burlap
against faded yellow oat shafts.

Something warm starts up, despite the tiredness of my body.
The mind and heart weaving future together,
like hot tea with sugar,
like daybreak over water, loons talking.
Warm things, like laughter in dreams.
Forever laughter from now on.

I shed his name like a used up skin.
Freedom twirls in my heart and flies,
pulsing with the locomotion of these tracks—
long iron rails into long iron rails.

Slow Bond

I feel the evidence of love in your touch.
I hear it in the language of your breath.
The integers of caring tumble over themselves
when you stand near, warm, next to me.

Our spirit-bodies greet one another in the morning.
Like the sun itself, spreading its fan over the Earth
and touching each grain of sand.

In the evening, our spirit-bodies want to lie down together
and rest in the same space.

Slot Canyon

Slot canyon buys my silence.
Fathoms deep, the spaces test my ingenuity
by erasing calculations.

The spaces give and get,
indecently at times.

I am watched on all sides by the grit.
Touched all over, by my own breath.
Licked clean by wind dancers.

I contort by necessity
in ways my spirit wills and my body obliges.

I step in and out of myself,
precise in my movements.

I make a small sound —
to break the spell.

I try not to disappear in the snake's throat
on this day.
Or let all realities melt helplessly
into one that snacks on me.

Sparrow

Down by the Ruby River, I hear your call—
a rustle in the leaves
and the long spiraling whistle.
The waters sigh over cobbles in agreement.

You say again that you love me,
that the Earth forgives,
And I listen—
wanting to believe you.

Speaking out

Heavy river,
naked fog,
landscaped people,
drizzly fence.

Trees hear.
Fingers understand.
Birch fidgets.

Spring

I could smell the torment of the river.
Fresh thaw stirred sediment as the sun melted.
The romance of heat died on the horizon
and oozed orange.

Your absence forced cold ripples in my chest.
The sex of summer heat stretched thin and disappeared.
Cedar waxwings froze in the paper birch
that struggled to send fresh growth into the world.

Serenity Washes Over

Cheeks tingling with salt air
rattle of black rocks
rubbing at the lighthouse beach.

Ocean
swishes, slurps through crevices
telling how small I am.

How small, how beautiful the heart—
floats up like a ghost and hovers
in awed silence.

Wind whirls strands of hair,
they fall in curves
like lines of tide on sand.

Stage for eternal whispers,
world beyond this floating heart,
beyond any touch of fingers on cold rocks,
beyond the stretch of eyes on the horizon.
Dimensions that swallow navigation
like the air swallows breath on a cold night.

Memories swallowed in time
like black rocks under surf.

Tide pushes closer and sucks back its eternal secrets.
Time has been invented—
the ghost-heart settles back in the body.

Black rocks are cold black rocks under feet.

Suck up

It is good
for a vacuum to bite its teeth into a rock.

It is good to tickle its bristles
with pine needles.

Go out, play, bring back the dirt.
Give the vacuum a good solid meal
instead of the empty fluff
of house dust and cookie crumbs.

Stehekin Winter

Sly river,
hiding between snow drifts,
humming under sheets of ice.

Creeks speak up while you hush your voice.
Moon glows on the snow blanket
you pull up to your chin.

Sun Mountain Lodge

Fog all the way to the ground.

Sound—
tapping, rapping, slapping
an uneasy rhythm from the eves.

Desert money on the fleshy leaves of lilies—
big lakes of dew.

Map of the world on a boulder.
aspens in fog shadows.

Christmas lights tangled in limbs.
Planned landscape wildness; illusion takes over.

Non-native plants sneak in the cracks of paved bricks.
Push.

Cool whisper.
Air stands close,
pressing fog in my cheeks.

Bolted wood pillars smell like sauna.
Yellow twig dogwood fooled
into pushing green leaves out
on Hallows eve.

Sundance Revelation

The drums are still in our feet.

Thunder beings roll across the sky
like 200 buffalo,
over the red dirt and into the river.

Lightening bolts. Light magnets.
Like the soul-talk of dancers
who look across the circle of sticks
and heal with a glance.
They are charmed by the tree.

My flesh is buried there. My sweat.
There is no burden on my back,
or chest, or tagged to my arms like feathers
or promises.

My hands are open
to receive the blessing of the wind.

My heart is beating the drum
of all my relations.

Swelling Stones

Fragile secrets passed between sisters.
A whisper, a look, a feeling
like string between hearts.
Even rocks would breathe,
bugs had names,
energy was ours.

Something changed when science gave answers.
So many questions dissolved.

Bugs became insects and arachnids,
energy slipped back in the earth.

Stones only breathe once in a while—
the vision is different.

And what of the string
stretched so far?
Will it break too?

The Canyon

Fingers of dust curled around her skin,
clutching her like a cloak,
owning her since the beginning of time.
The sky was gold as honey, the air sweet
and cool. Tumbling around her in cartwheels,
rolling the bushes, lifting her hair.

The electricity rose in her, and she stood
on the edge of the abyss, trying to make her eyes see further.
Trying to feel what was in the depths without falling in.

The clouds formed behind her in the distance,
and moved fast like shadows. Like a pack of wolves
drawn to her blood, they raced —
a dark group, tearing up the sky.

She could feel them coming.
She could see the dark swallowing the gold horizon.
The pulse of storm whipped through her and she leaned
as close to the deep as she could.

It was too late to see what was there.
She dangled her legs over the edge
and held her ground — dust powdering her hands.

The Cold Hardiness of Vegetables
--for my father

Again, the cherries bloom near the capitol
as I listen to a Ph.D from Michigan changing slides.
The cherries need pruning.

My fingers twitch, my back numb from sitting.
I yearn for the bonsai twig in my fingers.
The quiet snip in the buffered warmth of home.
My wife's footsteps on the stairwell.

The dwarfed cotoneaster branch is rough and fragile
like the leg of a bird I held for Dad
as he gently crimped the silver band.

The smell of tobacco was on his skin,
the earth in his nails.
Near us, the male killdeer took his turn
limping to protect granite eggs.
Mother always wondered how they hatched without warmth.
So much time spent protecting from a distance.

I notice the twisted paper branch in my fingers.
My mouth waters for tobacco.
I sneak a pinch to my lip in the dark—
salvation from slides of potatoes, turnips, test tubes.

My wife waits, dreaming of cherry blossoms.

The Shapes

Her circles from birth were strong
until Christianity gave them corners, edges.
She fought the box, but it pervaded.

Fair skin fit her in the grid;
expected her lines to be straight.

Experience stones piled up in her,
heavily round. They fell deep,
making waves. Circles in circles.

The Souls of Cedar Trees

Here the trees whisper of ancestors—
yours, mine, and everyone else's.
There is unity in the canopy,
the underground, and the in between.

We tiptoe over moss pillows.
Twiggy fingers reach out to touch our clothes.
Lichen fastens in our hair and rides along.

The soil is rich, good dirt,
and smells like the mouth of a cave.

The half-shelter of a house-sized boulder
draws us like magnets.

The sloughing bark of cedars
tempt our fingers to tug at the strips.
We hear water crackle through the canyon below,
blue as glacier ice.

Downed logs are slick but we crawl
over and under, on our backs,
or bellies, or knees.

Maneuvering is no trouble here,
under the giants.
Everything feels simple
in this small world under big trees.

Traveling

Where are you, dear one?
My bed is lonely without you.
My bare feet slide across gritty cotton sheets
to meet cold, empty, pockets of dark.

Your sleep-breathing and heat are in my memory alone.
The thought of your touch brings a smile to my lips.
My eyes open to see the imprint in the pillow
just as you left it.

The fan drums away at the air
in a quiet rhythm.
You are here in a ghostly way
And I can sleep.

Verga Dances

Ghost rain teases the backbone of a distant ridge
Like honey almost dripping from a spoon.
The sagebrush is pungent with anticipation—
powdery leaf bunches pursing like thirsty mouths.

Verga drops her pointed grey toes,
shyly, breathlessly, and dances pirouettes.
Parched clay crackles in awe and agony
while she flirts as lightly as a madrigal.
She seduces beads of sweat from dry earth,
cracked bark, parched leaves.

The sky dims and Verga sways
like the shadow of a bent branch
among piercing stars.
She boldly drops her cloak,
whispering showers that inebriate the land.

Sage, juniper, and dirt,
hang in the air like a flavor.
Verga laughs and lies down where she belongs.

Water Bonds

Our first kiss sent ripples wrapping round my spine
flapping 'round my toes like doves.

Something was perfect in that moment—
so perfect it couldn't be touched.
It was a drop of water
making craters of music in a pool.

We had found the molecular center.
We had captured the curved lattice bridge of art.

Bread Country Church

Choir voices waver
over fields of bearded wheat.

The old white church, artful and simple,
glows like a lantern over a grassy green sea.

A lone cottonwood clasps its leaves in the wind.

This is the easy season,
when the air smells of sweet clover
and woman sage.
When you taste the rain on your tongue
before the sky breaks open with a hammer.

A hundred years ago,
Lutherans bent their backs to the land
and built a place to come together
in a way we scarcely remember —
A handshake, a quiet word, a home.

Winter Morning

Naked river
clutches her terry cloth robe.

Winter teases the nape of her neck,
chilling down her spine
all the way to her flat feet.

Final Draft

My edges feel tattered
like an old quilt hung out to dry for too long
in the prairie wind.

Today is the last day
I will feel like crying without provocation.
I closed the book on a deadline that loomed
as thick as a bruised thundercloud.

Today I will breathe deep as a Yoga Master,
and isolate my mind from the vulgarities
of Microsoft Word.

First Day

Last night I dreamt of my Ph.D on a campus in the wilderness.
My room smelled sweet and fresh like cottonwood sap and
Douglas-fir needles.
My bed was on the limb of a tree.

The stone stairs were deliciously haphazard and mossy.
At the top, a meadow overlooked the river —
swirling blue with glacial flour.

"That is where you go to play," said my friend.
I saw the big river wave and the kayaks darting
in and out of its cradle and gliding over its ridge.

I imagine myself in a boat, riding the crest of the wave.
My heart was jubilant.

Then fear crept in. "I don't remember how," I said.
"Yes you do," he nodded, and I knew he was right.

I couldn't believe my fortune —
to be here, in the school of wilderness.
To witness beauty beyond measure and to learn with my eyes,
my heart, my hands, and my skin.

I was suddenly ready for the rest of my life.

Broken Wire

Circuits fire,
intentions fail
something needs mending.

Take my hand.
Be humble.
We will make the bridge together.

Tennis

Two bare feet
on the blue-green grit
of a tennis court floor.

White stripes gleam
like fog lines in the dusk.

Planned space.
Rectangles.
Netted all around
by wire diamonds of fence.

If I had a ball
I could hear that sound
when it pops hard against the slab
and keeps talking in the air.

Letting go

It is sad to think we are left behind
with only memories to hold with our hearts.

It hurts us not to have the power we need
to capture yesterday, or never reach tomorrow.

It is good to understand the time had come
for him to give his spirit to the maker of all hearts,
and consequently part from us.

But we will carry on—warmed
by his sturdy, subtle caring.
Sharing a bond with those he touched inside.

Winter Wren

Winter wren—
tiny, dull feathers,
Pavarotti in your song box.

Pierce the air with sound
and pump your tail.

So brave.
right up in my face.
Somersaulting in brush thickets.

God, you're beautiful.

New Start

Something has begun that feels different now
from all the times it has begun before.

One kiss fills me with anticipation
like the first rain on a crop of seeds.

The soil is thirsty,
the seeds nestle in,
and there is so much ahead
to be thankful for.

Fighting Fire with a Pulaski and a Smile

As I was swinging a Pulaski last weekend, to help the Glacier Institute rat-proof one of their cabins, I was reminded of my first big fire. It was several years back on the steep mountainsides of Idaho, and it had claimed hundreds of acres before a crew from Eureka, Montana was called in. I arrived late and didn't know what to expect. I had just stepped out of a bus and was walking through fire camp, looking for a crew from the Kootenai. The music of a chopper slapped its rhythm above us, dropping off two injured. In minutes, I was in the driver's seat of a van, listening to the doctor in the back saying, "can you hear me?" to a girl with second-degree burns. I spent the rest of my day in the hospital, waiting for news of a sawyer with broken ribs and a girl with burns who had passed out while I drove her to emergency. They were both stable, and we left the girl there to rest. The sawyer and doctor returned to camp with me.

I found my crew that night and unrolled my sleeping bag near their tarp shelter. It rained lightly most of the night, and I woke up wet before the sun came up. We ate platefuls of scrambled eggs and ham and piled into buses to ride to the site.

We could smell the smoke thick in the air before reaching it. Outside, we each carried the heavy weight of a full pack and a Pulaski or shovel in one hand, scaling the steep embankments. We passed a crew of sawyers from Ronan with big grins on their faces. I recognized my friend with broken ribs leaning against a tree, and he nodded shortly as I huffed by.

After two hours of uphill climbing, we reached our work-station and dug hand-line with pulaskis and shovels for the next ten hours, breaking in between to sit down and eat lunch for about five minutes. I switched my lead arm on my Pulaski regularly to keep from wearing one side out. I chopped at tree roots under the topsoil with my blade, and spun the handle to use to hoe-end for digging trench. Before long, my body was like a machine. On a hand line crew, it doesn't matter what you think or believe, it only matters how much you can dig and how long you can do it. The only viable complaint is a medical emergency. Even a grimace of crankiness from one worker will be answered by a glare from another.

We clocked out after fifteen hours. I found myself, at 9 p.m., trying to choose between two long lines of people. We looked like an army in the yellow shirts and green pants of Nomex fabric, leaning on one foot, then the other. I stared at each line — equally long — one for dinner and the other for showers. I desperately wanted both, but by the time I was through one line, the other would close down, they said. I opted for food.

We were all covered head to toe with a layer of grit and soot. Our bodies were clammy under our clothes and the whole camp reeked of sweat and smoke. By the time I got to the front of the line, they were getting low on food and we couldn't take as much as we were hungry for.

"Hurry up and eat," a cook said, "we want to get out of here."

At the time, it wasn't another insult, just another order. We wolfed down our food and smiled at her.

I stood in line for a shower too, holding the false hope that I might get one before they closed down for the night. I got lucky, and was in the last group of five women to shed our clothes and watch black streaks flush from our bodies and slither down the drain.

That night I hunkered down in my wet sleeping bag and slept, stone tired, until morning –which seemed to come around about twenty minutes later. We scrambled around for our gear in the dark and walked single file to the mess tent for breakfast.

Today my body aches in all the same places, as I roll out of a luxurious bed. I can remember the sting of smoke caked in my nostrils, but I can't feel it now. I think of all those firefighters in Arizona and New Mexico. Another fire season has begun. May their rocky beds be even, their food be generous, and may they come home safe and sound.

Wet Behind the Ears

They say a combat roll is just a start. Twenty years from now I'll be kissing the waves with my boat, smiling so much that it hurts. The first combat roll is an instant to remember. I can recall mine as if it were yesterday, because it very nearly was. The Middle Fork of the Flathead River in Montana will give me a smirk for years to come.

In the early afternoon, I slid my body into the spongy grip of Neoprene. A dozen other boaters did the same, suiting up in wetsuits, drysuits, and synthetic fleece, some of them finishing off early beers. The air was damp, and the chase of clouds—light and dark—was cat and mouse. At the put in, we shouldered our kayaks and took deep strides under the weight, our slippered and sandaled feet pushing tentative steps into the loose gravel.

I had been lifting weights in my living room, alone, toning my shoulders and back after my tiresome paddling two weekends before. At the water's edge, we squeezed into our cockpits, wiggled our toes, and shifted our knees into place against foam buffers inside. We watched the river go by—snow melt in transit—while we stretched spray skirts over the lip of combing on our cockpits.

I could feel a smile coming over me as my boat scraped sand, and I lifted my paddle to push. The still water of the eddy cradled my boat like a buoy. My paddle strokes were uncertain at first. I lingered in the comfort of the eddy, remembering how to ferry into the current and lean on the downriver side with my paddle to steady me. Easier said than done, I thought, beginning to try the maneuver. Kayaking tests the instincts of common sense, I had learned. To lean downriver is to do something stupid, if not fatal — this is how my mind churned as I took a deep breath and did it anyway.

The other boaters were right again; the steadier you lean, the better it works. Big waves can catapult a boat forward if the paddler knows how to use body weight and arms to work with the current and not against it.

At the first big rapid, water crashed over my hull and clapped against my face from all directions. I kept my hips loose and forgiving and my paddle strokes assertive through the white caps of "bone crusher" rapids. I stabbed my pointed bow into an eddy downstream to rest after an exhilarating ride.

Before each rapid, I listened carefully to the advice of boaters who knew this river like the blood in their veins. Stay left of center, paddle hard, take the eddy on river right, they advised. Part of me felt I should know this already. I had been over this before and was learning slowly. It didn't seem to matter. They smiled at me anyway, seeing the fresh excitement in my eyes. They wanted to share the rush of the sport without preening their egos. The river has low tolerance for a cocky approach, they had learned. The river, the almighty, can humble the best of the best.

Being underwater, upside-down, in a boat, is a curious experience — a rush of current and cold, a silence only the bubbles underneath can break through. As I clutched my paddle, I was vaguely aware of my actions — a sweep stroke, a snap of hips, bending back the wrist of my pivot arm. This motion tipped me up enough to gasp for air, one ear tuned to the thunder of water, the other deafened underneath. I knew, as I slid back under, that I would wet-exit and swim. The next time I would keep my head down and finish the sweep, I thought. Easier said than done.

The group of boaters darted in like sharks next to my body, eager to help.

"Grab my stern," one yelled. "Drop your boat," said another. They corralled my boat and urged it to shore, bumping its red sides with their bows. I kicked hard as another boater paddled cross-current to shore, dragging me on his stern grab loop. The water wrapped around me like ice and flushed from my clothing as I stood up in the cobbles. Shivering, I emptied my boat while my rescuers floated patiently in the eddy, ready to help if needed. There was only time enough for a few deep breaths, wringing my fleece hat and strapping my helmet down again. I couldn't make them wait. I slid squeakily into my boat, stretched the spray skirt into place, and was ready to paddle and get warm. We took gentle strokes on the moving water and my shivers died off just in time for the next wave train between rocks.

In the sluice of bubbles below the whitecaps, I slammed to the world underneath, the bubbles talking like laughter. Again, I was vaguely aware of my motions; the sweep, the snap of hips, the bend of wrist. A little voice said, "head down," and I resurfaced in a matter of seconds—my first combat roll. Water flushed from underneath my helmet, the heaviness of my wet hat close against my ears. I could hear the muffled yells of paddlers—cat calls and whoops—to celebrate my triumph.

Between the place where I rolled and the take out, I was able to look up at the hills without holding my breath. I noticed a bird sailing overhead, and the railroad snaking above us on the terrace. The green peaks of tree-covered hills surrounded us and the air was tangy with the smell of wild country. At the last bend before West Glacier, I looked up to see the old bridge arched like a backbone over the wide stretch of water. My crow's-feet wrinkles had deepened from smiling a good part of the day. I could hear the laughter of new friends above me on the bridge, trading stories and beers, catching the dim light of early September on their cheeks.

Dakota Prairie

The stretch of road rolled out before me like an amphibian tongue. I rested my weary head against my hand, the other gripping the wheel. A metropolis of clouds hung above me against the pale blue canvas of sky. I listened to the noise of road, whooshing and humming under my weight. The open fields; green and gold and brown, stretched across the land with the perfection of cultivated shapes. Despite what Mankind has done here, the land still echoes its spirit with authority. It quiets the traveler to introspection, and slows the heartbeat of time to the tempo of pulsing wind. Insects sing a relentless buzzing chorus in the grass. The birds own this place more than anything. The rest of us are just dots that move.

I had followed my gut feeling to get in the car and drive east toward my origins. I've spent most of my life west of the Rockies, but something beyond draws me like an umbilical to the rolling hills of western North Dakota, the badlands, the grassy dales and lake country of Minnesota. This is where it began, where I was a seed in the universe, waiting to form. The subtle shapes of this landscape string across the sky like wild animals in repose and I drink in their image and meditate on them. Nothing is real here. I couldn't imagine a daily life in this country. Getting up, going to work, shopping, going home to wash clothes. I see this place as a painting that graciously accepts me as I travel through it in four dimensions.

When I come home, the images last for a week and then begin to fade to pastel and fog—just enough memory to entice me next time I'm ready to journey to the spirit country, to the place of dreams. Perhaps only an artist or writer could understand the strange ways one gets inspiration. It's not that we understand, but we get a familiar feeling, the unexplained. We use a part of the rain that rests most of the time to draw on a seventh sense that guides and misguides us. Part of my journey was a quest to connect with relatives—lost connections that I wanted to rekindle. So much of our lives today ignore these things, but to me it was clear that connections define us, and our spiritual basis. I'm wary from the chase of insignificant things that control our days and disturb our nights. That's why I gassed up at the Fortine Merc in northwestern Montana and slipped onto the highway, free, headed toward Marias pass.

I drove long hours and slept very little. My first stop was a KOA campground in Havre to pitch a tent and sleep. The freight trains ran all night and I woke at dawn to drive another ten hours into the muggy west hills of North Dakota. Somehow this didn't bother me. Everything was just as it should be; nothing could touch me. I had no control over my journey except for where I was coming from and where I was going— the rest was a script I didn't have a copy of. I thought this way gleefully until I reached the stretch of chip rock that went on for 15-20 miles and grated like sand on my eardrums as I drove through it with hunched shoulders and pinched ears.

Dickinson, North Dakota, was my destination the second night. I stopped to visit my aunt, uncle and grandmother there and we talked all night. Their faces were glowing and animated. I felt at home, under familiar wings—although it had been years. We spent an active day in the tidy town of Dickinson. Perfect little houses line the streets with perfect rounded trees, and the train runs through twenty times a day with loads of Montana coal.

My third night was spent under a luminous sliver of moon. Jupiter was sparkling in the southern sky, and a vivid spin of clouds teased and turned up high. I stopped to see some friends and we stood outside, barefoot in the cool grass, watching shapes dance like northern lights. The air was sweet with clover and as dusk settled, the bats dove from the attic window of their creaky two-story house. We talked all night about nothing in particular and slept hard as stones. In the morning, we drove to the Mandan slant village at Fort Lincoln. I stood on the site of the Indian village and was drawn to different parts of the landscape by the tickle in my feet.

We had a quick lunch and I had another long day of driving ahead of me. It was another eleven hours to Circle Pines, a suburb of Minneapolis. The air was filled with storms and I chased dark clouds and lightening, then they chased me. I got a scratchy am station on the radio playing Muddy Waters and watched rain pelt designs in the windshield. Tears flushed across my cheeks and I began to laugh. I felt so small, like a little bug in a little tiny car, scooting across the landscape of Earth, one little speck in the universe.

The lake country was shrouded in darkness as I snuck in among the other cars, rumbling along at seventy miles per hour. I dodged traffic and pushed into the flow where my exits gaped like concrete mouths. At Circle Pines, the traffic slowed. I ducked into Golden Lake road and could smell the water. I was closing in on my furthest point east, the home of my uncle and aunt. My tires gripped the night pavement, rolling to a stop where there lights glimmered in the doorway.

I stepped across the threshold an entered the room where they sat. They regarded me cautiously, seeing that I had been somewhere I couldn't shake off. The road had owned me and I had owned it. My eyes were heavily weary, my hands quivering from motion, my body starved. I sat down and they waited for me to come around.

We moved to the sunken room where everyone talks and I sat in my place, one spoke of the web that stretched between us. We talked about journeys, and dreams, and past lives we'd had and how much we'd changed. We talked until two and when I woke up, I was happy.

Wear and Tear on a Road Gypsy

8 miles west of Snowville, Idaho

Two wedding rings jangle around my neck like bells as I trot through a grove of juniper trees. Blue, my dog, thunders from behind to catch me, tongue lolling, mouth open in a smile. The air is too cold for shorts, and goose bumps rise across my legs. I look at my wheels and smile. A grey 89 Isuzu Trooper, dinged, rusted, cracked on the windshield, and seen 146,000 miles. I feel about the same. The bit that makes me smile is the red kayak on top—perched like a gem with a sleek handmade wooden paddle. On this trip I am only taking what I need, and I need this. Another 600 miles of road and the thought of sliding my boat into the Dolores River inspires me. For the first time in months, I am happy.

I thought the rings would feel heavy, like two pieces of lead I would carry like a martyr. Instead, the weight is amiable and the sound of gold and diamonds delightful like chimes.

The miles pass by in daydreams. As I get close to the Canyonlands, shadows of the past press in and make me small. I can feel my heart like a warm but empty cup. I indulge my sorrow, letting the film reels roll. I think of the moment I gave my heart away on a mesa above Green River Canyon, sun falling, moon rising, wind tickling up my satin dress. I was the moon—full, vulnerable and magnetic. I pulled his heart like the oceans and he pulled mine. Until then, I had never really done it. Never totally offered my heart for the taking.

In Moab, Utah, the air is hot and heavy and carries the pulse of a lizard. The noontime social scene—thriving with Tevawearing, whitewashed outdoor enthusiasts—chatters on but the pulse is low and thready, making thirst ache in my throat. I order my tofu pita and shuffle to the corner, thinking about how I could go look up my name, and his, at the courthouse. I don't, of course. I let the sun bake the heartbreak out of me.

After food, I'm better. I'm still smiling more than I have in a very long time, and I can feel the Dolores talking to me from miles away. I can imagine a cool breeze writhing down the canyon, pushing willows into a dance. The country gives me a silly grin—open, sunbaked sandstone, broccoli trees, sage. Windswept openness with delicious snowy peaks puncturing the sky, and the full-bodied mesas, tilted, angled, wise.

The vision pleases me, and I wonder exactly why I might feel so giddy after being emotionally bulldozed. I decide it's mostly that I lived. I survived a spell of darkness, and I can smell, see, eat, hear, and speak above a whisper once again. I see Sleeping Ute Mountain ahead of me—the beautiful silhouette in repose.

My toes tingle for solid ground after months of vagrancy. Dolores, Colorado is a good place to hang my keys. I love the road but need a niche—a place to lay my bedroll and call my own. I am afraid to love the place too much. I have mending to do before I can plant flowers and pretend, but the river tempts me. The river sweet-talks like a new kind of lover.

Skagit Winter

This morning, the maples wrecked my heart with beauty. They glowed like spun gold against an azure sky. Now the grass is bending low, whispering, and the cohos are sticking to the ribs of the river. There are men in brown neoprene bibs tossing their lures across the water. A hawk and two crows bicker for air territory over the brown grass. Winter is on the wing. Soon the eagles will bring their cousins.

The eagles come here by the hundreds. Last year, between November and February, the high count was over five hundred and fifty along the scenic stretch of the Skagit River between Marblemount and Mount Vernon, Washington. In fact, in any given day during the months of November to February, there were more eagles than eagle watchers.

The salmon slide on their bellies across the rounded river gravels polished by glaciers. The salmon journey home as they have for hundreds of years past obstacles, predators, and prey. They lose their appetites and their flesh as they dance through glacier-fed waters, pulsing their tails above Skagit green schist.

I ride my bike with my four-legged companion; a stub-tailed, devoted blue heeler. We take the "new" road, paved with glacial till, to the spawning channel that parallels the river. This sandy pseudo-natural dike gives salmon, and their fry, a safe haven. It is a clean, aerated, slow-moving place for eggs to mature and begin a new life cycle. I pause on the footbridge and look down on a graying chum. Seven species of anadromous fish travel to this stretch of river. A powerful snap, snap of the tail and this aging beauty is upstream of me, in the shelter of fallen branches. Overhead, an eagle pulses its wings on air. My home; a short walk from this channel, lies on the flight path between two drop-dead-gorgeous rivers, the Cascade and the

Skagit. Both are scenic, wild, and painfully cold. And both create a seasonal refuge for hundreds of showy bald eagles. It is their southern winter home. Flying south, for them, is a journey from one jagged range of mountains to another, from Alaska to Washington. I consider my parallel journey.

The first time I was awestruck by eagles, salmon, and the habitat they share, was near Ketchikan, Alaska. I spent a summer pulling three scales each from coho and sockeye in a remote Forest Service camp in the Misty Fiords. I pressed each scale into a notebook with tweezers; identified sex and species, then cradled each fish in Bakewell Creek, watching for signs of revival. With fresh water in their gills it didn't take long for them to shake off the drowsy effects of MS-222, a water-soluble fish relaxant. At night we would hear the newcomers rattle the trap—feisty wallops against the steel bars that contained them. The Forest Service had built a fish ladder that routed salmon around a 40-foot waterfall to our trap. They swam from the Pacific Ocean, to Bakewell Arm, to Bakewell Creek, up the ladder and through the woods to Bakewell Camp, and a foreign cage. We did our best to cycle them through as quickly as possible, but we had to wait for the sun to rise. And when it did, we were in the most beautiful place on earth with the talk of the creek as our constant company.

The coho were especially feisty. I would cradle each fish, rocking forward and back to pass fresh water through the gills. Suddenly, a slap of cold slippery tail against my bare forearm left a tingling wet rush and another salmon fled to freedom.

The eagle comes by again, in the opposite direction. The chum wanders in and out of a sandy gully. The timing between this predator and prey is unique. Eagle waits for the end of the life cycle, biding her time in the top of a bare maple. Along the river and in side streams the salmon lay and fertilize eggs, then roll listlessly onto cobble bars or sink to the sand where eagles feast and flap like schoolyard crows.

Each time I am on the Skagit River in winter, by raft or kayak, I sense the pulse of connectedness like a slap to the arm. My awareness opens. When I am on the river I have a deep sense that I am on the right road. I reflect that it was the only road into this country for many thousand years. Here, the salmon descendants pass beneath my boat, determined to begin the next generation of fry, just as ancient salmon passed beneath the dugout canoes of human ancestors.

My blue heeler and I turn to ride the cobbles homeward. I take my lesson from the persistence of salmon, through all obstacles, pushing on, finding the place where beginning meets end. Eagles, whose paths of flight are increasingly encroached upon, also continue a migratory tradition. My comprehension of the struggle for all species is drowsy and unfocused like a cradled fish. So many of our rivers are challenged by unnatural forces yet here life cycles are still tangible from my front door in these glacier-fed streams. The Skagit River seems wild in this stretch of river and the Cascade River is unencumbered by dams. Both are surrounded largely by wilderness at their headwaters and for much of their reach.

Today's upriver fishermen stand in the water—Neoprene clad. Poles, zippers, flies, hooks, velcro. They squish water between their toes and climb into Toyotas, Mazdas and Fords. They drive home for a hot shower and a faded pair of sweat pants.

Today no hand woven nets or weirs made of cedar, willow, and river cobbles, hold fast in the current. Dugout cedar canoes no longer grace the Upper Skagit or the Cascade Rivers. No more diamond-head or square-headed paddles, hand-hewn with stone chisels, dip into these home waters. No canoe poles press to the floor of the river, pushing boats against current from one eddy to another, one camp to another one country to another, one generation to another.

In a few key places, the people of the Skagit lay their nets and floats. This is one privilege granted to continue a tradition. Some fish are sold, and some are smoked over an alder fire. Many are integrated into modern ceremony. Everyone brings containers. Everyone eats.

The rivers seem lonesome for the songs of salmon and eagles and sustenance. Ancestral fisherman, nearly 10,000 years of them, knew persistence, humility, cycles, and seasons. Thankfulness. Our lessons are not all behind us. We must remember and push on, with hope and purpose, to what lies ahead.

As the Skagit flows toward its delta, the river flattens and winds through small towns and past cabins. Past hillsides raw from timber harvest, between agricultural fields, cows, and alongside a state highway. The Skagit River grazes bridge abutments and flows beneath power lines, and alongside hundreds of culverts and homes; neighborhoods. It separates the mall from the Macdonald's. It flows under the Interstate, to the delta, to the bay.

Salmon pass one another at the mouth of the river and eagles glide through a sea of seagulls, looking for a perch. Jets fly over casinos, rest stops, estuaries, gas stations, backhoes, barns, and substations. They cruise over lush green islands and arid, blacktop parking lots, stacks of logs, lawns, landfills.

Salmon cross the ocean on a sacred journey. They leave the buoyancy of saltwater for the firm push of glacial melt. They smell their way to the mouth of the river, sensing the vibration of stones, remembering that place where everything began. They meditate and fast. Their bodies scrape against the beds of rivers and creeks. They focus and persist. They push upriver, toward home.